I'll get my Jacket

Good, and shut the door on your way out!

Steven William Park

Ukiyoto Publishing

All global publishing rights are held by

Ukiyoto Publishing

Published in 2022
Content Copyright © Steven William Park

ISBN 9789364947770

All rights reserved.

No part of this publication may be reproduced, transmitted, or stored in a retrieval system, in any form by any means, electronic, mechanical, photocopying, recording or otherwise, without the prior permission of the publisher.

The moral rights of the author have been asserted.

This is a work of fiction. Names, characters, businesses, places, events, locales, and incidents are either the products of the author's imagination or used in a fictitious manner. Any resemblance to actual persons, living or dead, or actual events is purely coincidental.

This book is sold subject to the condition that it shall not by way of trade or otherwise, be lent, resold, hired out or otherwise circulated, without the publisher's prior consent, in any form of binding or cover other than that in which it is published.

www.ukiyoto.com

For all my Family wherever they are

I went to the music store at the weekend and asked if they had anything by The Doors…
The guy behind the counter said; "Yes, a fire extinguisher and an umbrella stand"

When I sing Frank Sinatra songs, everyone's always keen to point out the errors of My ways

---

My girlfriend announced over breakfast that she's leaving me because she says I'm obsessed with twitter...
I nearly choked on my #Brown

"Frank Sinatra has eaten most types of bird."
"Egrets?"
"He's had a few"

Has anyone seen my Wife? I think she left me because of my obsession with Pantomimes
My neighbours told me she was across the road.
I said, "Oh no she isn't "

I once got so drunk I fixed my dartboard to the ceiling...
Spent the rest of the night throwing up!

Saw two fellas in the village working round the park. One was digging holes then the other one just filled it in.
I said, "what are you doing?"
They said there should be three of them but the bloke who plants the trees is off sick

---

If you have back pain in Egypt, would you see a Cairo practor

---

I once entered the world kleptomaniac championships, I took gold, silver and bronze.

I made a lovely wedding cake for a friend and was so upset when someone stole the top layers...
I was reduced two tiers.

My wife's started decorating the living room in some kind of gothic horror theme.
Skull design curtains, a devil's face throw etc.
I'm worried there'll be grim reaper cushions.

I went to a restaurant last night. I ordered a salad.
As soon as the waiter brought it, a man came over, snatched it and ran away.
I shouldn't have ordered a seize a salad.

Local Police hunting the 'knitting needle nutter' who has stabbed six people in the arse in the last 48 hours, believe the attacker could be following some kind of pattern.
Trust me they do get worse!

How do you know when a Gorilla is Poor?
He hasn't got two Ape Knees to rub together!

I was watching the film version of Cats and half the audience walked out.
That's unusual for an inflight movie.

Went to a University Challenge theme restaurant the other day. The main courses were very expensive, over thirty pounds, but I had a starter for ten.

My first car was so old; it took part in the Battle of Hastings…
It was a Triumph Harold.

I've just been to hospital because I tripped over a box of Kleenex.
I'm OK. though, it was just a soft tissue injury.

I think it's a disgrace on society and our education system when after 50 years, most people have no idea who Neil Armstrong is.
Or what kind of trumpet he played

I got a pet newt, and I named him Tiny.
Because he's my newt.

I'm currently watching the film "A Fistful Of French Sticks".
It's a Baguettey Western

"Did you have a mince pie Julius?"
"Et tu Brute!"

Why do people never admit to being just the right amount of whelmed...?

I've just finished converting my car to electric, I swapped the engine for the motor from a tumble dryer. It wouldn't start at first, then I realized I hadn't shut the door properly.

The wife just threw some fabric softener at me. It must have been lenor because it was too close for comfort.

My wife and I were watching Who Wants to Be A Millionaire while we were in bed.
I turned to her and said, 'Do you want to have Sex?'
'No,' she answered.
I then said, 'Is that your final answer?'
She didn't even look at me this time, simply saying, 'Yes'
So I said, "Then I'd like to phone a friend."
And that's when the fight started.

I took my wife to a restaurant. The waiter, for some reason, took my order first.
"I'll have the rump steak, rare, please."
He said, "Aren't you worried about the mad cow?"
"Nah, she can order for herself."
And that's when the fight started...

My wife and I were sitting at a table at her high school reunion, and she kept staring at a drunken man swigging his drink as he sat alone at a nearby table.
I asked her, "Do you know him?" "Yes", she sighed, "He's my old boyfriend. I understand he took to drinking right after we split up those many years ago, and I hear he hasn't been sober since."
"My God!" I said, "Who would think a person could go on celebrating that long?"
And then the fight started

It's perfectly fine for the cat to take off and hide under the couch when we have visitors.
When I do it, It's suddenly 'Anti social'

When I was a kid I got thrown out of the sea scouts because my tent sank.

So at our local chippy, they still use old newspaper to wrap up their fish and chips.
Yesterday I got a plaice in the sun.

Just bought the wife a novelty telephone in the shape of a dog.
It's a Golden Receiver.

I misunderstood 'Pride month'
Does anyone want 14 lions?

The man who invented the needle and thread is critically ill in hospital.
Doctors warn it's unlikely he'll pull through.

When our lawn mower broke and wouldn't run, my wife kept hinting to me that I should get it fixed. But, somehow I always had something else to take care of first, the shed, the boat, making beer.. Always something more important to me.

Finally, she thought of a clever way to make her point. When I arrived home one day, I found her seated in the tall grass, busily snipping away with a tiny pair of sewing scissors. I watched silently for a short time and then went into the house. I was gone only a minute, and when I came out again I handed her a toothbrush. I said, "When you finish cutting the grass, you might as well sweep the driveway."

The doctors say I will walk again, but I will always have a limp.

My wife sat down next to me as I was flipping channels.
She asked, "What's on TV?"
I said, "Dust."
And then the fight started...

My wife was hinting about what she wanted for our upcoming anniversary.
She said, "I want something shiny that goes from 0 to 150 in about 3 seconds."
I bought her a bathroom scale.
And then the fight started......

I'll get my Jacket

Saturday morning, I got up early, quietly dressed, made my lunch, and slipped quietly into the garage. I hooked up the boat up to the van and proceeded to back out into a torrential downpour. The wind was blowing 50 mph, so I pulled back into the garage, turned on the radio, and discovered that the weather would be bad all day.

I went back into the house, quietly undressed, and slipped back into bed. I cuddled up to my wife's back; now with a different anticipation, and whispered, "The weather out there is terrible."

My loving wife of 5 years replied, "And, can you believe my stupid husband is out fishing in that?"

And that's how the fight started...

After retiring, I went to the Social Security office to apply for Social Security. The woman behind the counter asked me for my driver's License to verify my age. I looked in my pockets and realized I had left my wallet at home. I told the woman that I was very sorry, but I would have to go home and come back later.

The woman said, 'Unbutton your shirt'. so I opened my shirt revealing my curly silver hair. She said, 'That silver hair on your chest is proof enough for me' and she processed my Social Security application. When I got home, I excitedly told my wife about my experience at the Social Security office.

She said, 'You should have dropped your pants. You might have gotten disability too.'

And then the fight started...

My wife was standing nude, looking in the bedroom mirror.
She was not happy with what she saw and said to me, "I feel horrible; I look old, fat and ugly. I really need you to pay me a compliment.'
I replied, "Your eyesight's damn near perfect."
And then the fight started........

I rear-ended a car this morning...the start of a REALLY bad day!
The driver got out of the other car, and he was a DWARF!!
He looked up at me and said 'I am NOT Happy!'
So I said, 'Well, which one ARE you then?'

That's how the fight started.

When I was younger I was scared of the dark........
but now when I see my electricity bill I am scared of the lights!!
One year, I decided to buy my mother-in-law a cemetery plot
as a Christmas gift...
The next year, I didn't buy her a gift.
When she asked me why, I replied,

"Well, you still haven't used the gift I bought you last year!"
And that's how the fight started.

My local football team have signed a Centre Forward called Jack.
Apparently he's great in the box

Just been to B & Q and the wife has got a ladder in her tights.
She's an amazing shoplifter.

Have you ever got halfway through eating a horse and thought…
'I'm not as hungry as I thought I was?'

I saw a snake slithering across the windows of my Volkswagen.
I'm not an expert, but I'm pretty sure it was a vindscreen viper.

My mum has been charged with drinking out of date coffee cream liqueur. The trial is set for the Old Bailey's.

I have a really exciting job. I wear a white Stetson hat, ride a white horse, wear a mask and right the wrongs of the world with my faithful sidekick, Tonto.
Well....that's a bit of exaggeration....
I'm only a mortgage advisor, really.

I really wish I'd known the guy next door was a retired hit man, before I asked him to take the dog out!
This morning, after 25 years' use, my clothes horse broke beyond repair.
It's the end of an airer.

During a company's recent password audit the following password came to light:
"MickeyMinniePlutoHueyLouieDeweyDonaldGoofyBerlin".
When the employee was asked why he had such a long password, he said,
"I was told it had contain at least 8 characters and include one capital"

I pressed the plunger on my cafeteria this morning and the Starbucks across the road exploded.

This will be our first Christmas dinner without grandad, but we know he'll be up there looking down on us as we tuck in.
It's his own fault for breaking his stair lift.

My calculator has suddenly stopped working.
Something doesn't add up here.

Whilst Alan Turing was decoding the Enigma machine, his sister Kay was busy making tea and sandwiches.

A man was seriously injured yesterday when his homemade bookcase fell on him.
He only has his shelf to blame.
Mariah Carey doesn't want turkey, all she wants for Christmas is stew!

As a Child -You're Grounded!
As an Adult -Your package will be delivered between 8am and 6pm.

Tonight we are going to the Amateur Ventriloquist Society's Christmas Gall.

My next door Neighbour knocked on my door we just wearing a see through Negligee, asked to borrow a cup of sugar, and then winked at me and asked to come in for a cup of coffee. I said :Fuck off Dave!"

Me and my exceptionally flat chested wife went to see a marriage counsellor today. The counsellor asked us; "What seems to be the problem?" "Well," I said, "Dolly Parton here thinks I'm too sarcastic'

Today I bought my wife a false leg for Christmas. It's not her main present, it's just a stocking filler.

Once again this year I've had requests for my Vodka Christmas Cake recipe, so here goes. Made mine this morning!
1 cup sugar, 2 mugs of flour , 1 tsp baking powder, 1 cup water, 1 tsp salt, 1 cup brown sugar, lemon juice, 4 large eggs, nuts, 1...bottle Vodka, 2 cups dried fruit.
Sample a cup of Vodka to check quality. Take a large bowl, check the Vodka again to be sure it is of the highest quality, then repeat. Turn on the electric mixer. Beat one cup of butter in a large fluffy bowl. Add 1 teaspoon of sugar. Beat again.
At this point, it is best to make sure the Vodka is still okay. Try another cup just in case. Turn off the mixer thingy. Break 2 eggs and add to the bowl and chuck in the cup of dried fruit.
Pick the fruit up off the floor, wash it and put it in the bowl a piece at a time trying to count it. Mix on the turner. If the fried druit gets stuck in the beaters, just pry it loose with a drewscriver.

Sample the Vodka to test for tonsisticity. Next, sift 2 cups of salt & 2 mugs of flower, or something. Check the Vodka. Now sh!t the lemon juice and strain your nuts. Add one table. Add a spoon of sugar, or somefink. Whatever you can find.

Greash the oven. Turn the cake tin 360 degrees and try not to fall over. Don't forget to beat off the turner. Finally, throw the bowl through the window. Finish the Vodka and wipe the counter with the cat.

Dracula goes to Rome for a holiday, at his hotel he orders room service. Girl brings him a tray of goodies. Old Drac ignores the tray, grabs the girl, bites her on the neck sucks her dry and tosses the empty skin out of the window. He reorders the same from room service and grabs the girl bites her on the neck, sucks her dry and tosses the empty skin out of the window.

Dracula is having a good old time grabbing people passing his room, Biting them on the neck, sucking them dry and tossing the empty skins out of the window.

In the cafe outside I saw Sacha Distel sitting drinking a coffee, I said Hello Sacha How are things... He replied " Oh ok except that 'Drained wops keep falling on my head

---

I was walking down the road when I saw an Afghan bloke standing on a fifth floor balcony shaking a carpet. I shouted up to him, "What's up Abdul, won't it start?"

My friend then said to me "You lousy sod, I'd have offered to at least give him a push to get it going."

Mary Poppins was travelling home but due to worsening weather, she decided to stop at a hotel for the night. She approached the receptionist and asked for a room for the night:
"Certainly madam." He replied courteously.
"Is the restaurant open still?" Enquired Mary.
"Sorry, no." Came the reply. "But room service is available all night. Would you care to select something from this menu?"
Mary smiled and took the menu and perused it.
"Hmm, I would like cauliflower cheese please," said Mary.
"Certainly, madam." He replied.
"And can I have breakfast in bed?" Asked Mary politely.
The receptionist nodded and smiled.
"In that case, I would love a couple of poached eggs, please." Mary mused.
After confirming the order, Mary signed in and went up to her room for the night.
The night passed uneventfully and the next morning Mary came down early to check out. The same guy was still on the desk.
"Morning madam, did you sleep well?"

"Yes, thank you." Mary replied.
"Was the food to your liking?"
"Well, I have to say the cauliflower cheese was exceptional, I don't think I have had better. Shame about the eggs, though, they really weren't that nice at all." Replied Mary truthfully.
"Oh,well, perhaps you could contribute these thoughts to our Guest Comments Book. We are always looking to improve our service and would value your opinion." Said the receptionist.
"OK, I will...thanks!" Replied Mary, who checked out, then scribbled a comment into the book. Waving, she left to continue her journey.
Curious, the receptionist picked up the book to see the comment Mary had written!
"Supercauliflowercheesebuteggswerequiteatrocious!"

It's been Months since I ordered the book "How to scam people online: It hasn't arrived as yet!

A few years ago my mate had a bone marrow transplant, he said luckily they found a match in Argentina. He said I will always be grateful to deago marrow donor.

Did you know that Bruce Lee had a vegan brother?
Broco Lee.

I couldn't get my jogging trousers off yesterday... the doctor says I need an emergency trackybottomy

---

If Sherlock Holmes was a teacher, he would teach in elementary school.

A man was rushed to hospital after choking on a handful of chocolate coated toffees, orange crèmes and raisins.
He was pronounced dead on a Revel.

I went to an Indian restaurant last night. After I had ordered, a little old lady came to me and said, "Aren't you polite. You have such lovely manners."
Apparently, it was my complimentary nan.

I stopped at a very upmarket burger van yesterday.
It had 4 Michelin tyres.

Paddy goes to a florist & says "I'd like to buy some flowers for my girlfriend."

The florist says "Certainly, what is it you're after?"
Paddy says "A tit wank"

Just got my hair cut -My wife says it's terrible but I thought it was OK - guess I shall have to Mullet over

---

I think my doctor liked my choice of footwear, I heard him telling his colleagues that I had serious healthy shoes

My wife told me that sex is better on vacation. It wasn't the best postcard I've ever received.

Facts of life for the elder Generation:
1. When one door closes and another door opens, you are probably in prison.
2. To me, "drink responsibly" means don't spill it.
3. Age 60 might be the new 40, but 9:00 pm is the new midnight.
4. It's the start of a brand new day, and I'm off like a herd of turtles.
5. The older I get, the earlier it gets late.
6. When I say, "The other day," I could be referring to any time between yesterday and 15 years ago.
7. I remember being able to get up without making sound effects.
8. I had my patience tested. I'm negative.

9. Remember, if you lose a sock in the dryer, it comes back as a Tupperware lid that doesn't fit any of your containers.

10. If you're sitting in public and a stranger takes the seat next to you, just stare straight ahead and say, "Did you bring the money?"

11. When you ask me what I am doing today, and I say "nothing," it does not mean I am free. It means I am doing nothing.

12. I finally got eight hours of sleep. It took me three days, but whatever.

13. I run like the winded.

14. I hate when a couple argues in public, and I missed the beginning and don't know whose side I'm on.

15. When someone asks what I did over the weekend, I squint and ask, "Why, what did you hear?"

16. When you do squats, are your knees supposed to sound like a goat chewing on an aluminum can stuffed with celery?

17. I don't mean to interrupt people. I just randomly remember things and get really excited.

18. When I ask for directions, please don't use words like "east."

19. Don't bother walking a mile in my shoes. That would be boring. Spend 30 seconds in my head. That'll freak you right out.

20. Sometimes, someone unexpected comes into your life out of nowhere, makes your heart race, and changes you forever. We call those people cops.

21. My luck is like a bald guy who just won a comb.

I'm thinking of starting a hokey cokey appreciation society
Are you in or out?

I've just changed all the light bulbs in the house to 3 watt.
My wife's taken a very dim view.

Just been sacked from my job at the pet shop.
Got caught with my hand in the Trill.

How do you console an English Teacher?
There, their, they're.

If Satan ever lost his hair, there would be all hell toupée?

Paddy had long heard the stories of an amazing family tradition.
It seems that his father, grandfather and great-grandfather had all been able to walk on water on their 18th birthday.
On that special day, they'd each walked across the lake to the pub on the far side for their first legal drink.

So when Paddy's 18th birthday came around, he and his pal Mick took a boat out to the middle of the lake, Paddy, stepped out of the boat ... and nearly drowned! Mick just barely managed to pull him to safety.

Furious and confused, Paddy went to see his grandmother...

"Grandma he asked, "Tis me 18th birthday, so why can't I walk across the lake like me father, his father and his father before him?"

Granny looked deeply into Paddy's, troubled eyes and said, "Because ye father, ye grandfather and ye great-grandfather were all born in December when the lake is frozen, and ye were born in August, ya fekin idiot!"

Hey guy's listen up. Tell the ladies in your life that Tesco are handing out free holly and mistletoe when you buy tampax, lillets etc this month. But hurry, it's just for the Christmas period.

I accidentally fell into a vat of fluorescent paint.
Been sent home from hospital for complete rest and time to reflect.

Paddy phones an ambulance because his mate's been hit by a car.
Paddy: 'Get an ambulance here quick, he's bleeding from his nose and ears and I tink both his legs are broken.'

I'll get my Jacket

Operator: 'What is your location sir?'
Paddy: 'Outside number 28 Eucalyptus Street.'
Operator: 'How do you spell that sir?'
Silence.... (heavy breathing) and after a minute.
Operator: 'Are you their sir?'
More heavy breathing and another minute later.
Operator: 'Sir, can you hear me?'
This goes on for another few minutes until....
Operator: 'Sir, please answer me. Can you still hear me?'
Paddy: 'Yes, sorry bout dat... I couldn't spell eucalyptus, so I just dragged him round to number 3 Oak Street.

In the pub I was talking to a guy who said he was going to buy his mistress two presents this year. "A diamond ring, and a sports car"
He said "If she doesn't like the ring, she can drive to the jewelers and change it"
I replied that I was going to buy my wife two presents also. "A pair of slippers and a dildo"
If she doesn't like the slippers, she can go fuck herself!

I called the Vets this morning
Me: Hello I'd like to make an appointment for my Pet Ostrich please.
Vet: Ok, what seems to be the problem?
Me: He seems to be holding his neck to one side.
Vet: Hmm I see, maybe necks weak.
Me: Haven't you got anything sooner?

The brewery I work for as their National Sales Manager have decided to reduce my role.
I am now their National Ales Manager.

I used to test people's eyes for a living and I really thought they would never fail.
I was the eternal optometrist..

My mate just phoned me to tell me he had changed his name by deed poll to Spinal Column.
I said, "Can I call you back?"

The donkeys at the seaside are going to be replaced by camels.
Do you know what the camels are getting for lunch?
The same as the donkeys, half an hour.

Me and my wife have found the secret of a happy marriage is to never to have puzzle books in the house.
10 years and not a crossword between us.

I tried a new shampoo today... At first I was surprised but then I felt a profound sense of sorrow. It's called Gosh & Woe.

At Christmas we were so hard up. We got a packet of batteries with a note saying toys not included.

Did you hear about the woolly Xmas gift hat Bing Crosby got from David Bowie?
It was a proper pom pom.

Someone wanted to swap their leprechaun for one of Santa's reindeer, but I told them I wouldn't take gnome for a Prancer.

Thanks to whoever posted the Christmas card through today, with the word 'Copious' written inside. It means a lot.

I picked up a fare in London and was asked to drive him to 221b Baker Street.
Looks like I'm driving Holmes for Christmas.

At this time of year, there's nothing I love more than sitting in front of a warm fire, mulled wine in hand, and singing Christmas songs until I slowly fall asleep.
And that's why I'm no longer a fireman.

Santa wouldn't allow his elves to talk in the workshop. They could chat in the marquees where the gifts were stored.

They couldn't discuss the future or the past... they could only talk in the present tents.

Hoping my mate's girlfriend gets back from Ukraine before the 25th. No one wants a chick in Kiev for Christmas.

Very proud of my son; he's been studying sugar production at university and has just granulated.

I tried to teach my dog to dance today...He was useless.

He's got 2 left feet.

I used to work solo, granting mortgages.

I was the Loan Arranger.

You can tell if someone likes fine china by holding a better cup under their chin.

"Dear Agony Aunt Deirdre, my wife doesn't understand me... She's Russian!"

How did Mary and Joseph get their groceries delivered?

On a Lidl donkey.

I've decided my 2022 new year's resolution is going to be to give up using aerosol deodorant. Roll on January 1st.

Welcome to Assumptions Group. I think we all know why we're here.

I come from a very musical family, even my mums sewing machine was a singer

---

It's been pretty grim in the electronics industry the last few months. But we must solder on.

I've heard a well-known dog food manufacturers are in financial difficulties; they've had to call in the retrievers.

SCAM ALERT: Crabs have been wandering the streets with hip flasks of whisky asking if people fancy a nip.

Don't fall for it.

A bit of useless information for you. I was an extra on Dirty Dancing. I had the time of my life.

A Freudian slip is when you say one thing but mean your mother.....I mean another.

I've been having a good go at varnishing some old furniture without too much success... but it hasn't been for the lacquer trying!

I was walking down the street said to my younger mate," Hey, doesn't that bloke look like Tommy Cooper.

My mate said, "He's before my time, what did he look like?"

I pointed at the bloke and said, "Just like that."

I used to eat a lot of natural foods until I learned that most people die of natural causes.

I was on a pony trek once and the leader asked me if I could shoe a horse…I said 'I'll give it a go … after all I once told a donkey to clear off.'

A child asked his Father "How were people born?" So his Father said, "Adam and Eve made babies, then their babies grew up and they had babies… and so on" The child then went to his Mother and asked the same question. His Mother replied

"We were Monkeys, then we evolved to become what we are now." The Boy ran back to his Father and said "You lied to me!" The Father replied "No I didn't, your Mother was talking about her side of the Family!"

A bit of useless information for you. I was an extra on Dirty Dancing. I had the time of my life.

It is a five-minute walk from my home to the pub. But it is 35 minutes to get home. The difference is staggering.

Important facts to remember as you grow older:

1:   Death is the number one killer in the World.

2:   Life is sexually transmitted.

3:   Good health is merely the slowest rate at which one can die.

4:   Men have only two emotions Hunger and Horny and they cannot tell them apart. If you see a gleam in his eye, make him a sandwich. You have a 50%chance of being right.

5:   Teach a person to fish and you feed them for a day. Teach them how to use the internet and you won't see them for days, weeks even months.

6:   Healthy nuts are going to feel stupid someday. Laying in a Hospital bed, dying of nothing.

7:   All of us could tale a lesson from the weather, it pays no attention to criticism:

8.   In the '60s, people took acid to make the world look weird. Now the World is weird, people now take Prozac to make it look normal.

9:   Life is like a jar of Jalapeno peppers. What you might do today might burn your arse tomorrow,

10: Don't worry about old age, it does not last that long.

At Last I can make a woman go weak at the tremble all over. Thanks for the Taser for my Darling wife.

The Pessimist sees the glass as half empty.

The Optimist see the glass as half full.

The Realist knows either way there is room for gin or Bacardi!

I've just been to a pet shop and asked shoul dog a tin of Food or a bone.

He said "What's the dog's name?"

I said "Nic Nac Paddy Whack"

I took my horse to the vets the other day be a hole in it. The vet told me there was noth about this as it was a polo pony.

I thought it was the tumble dryer that was shrinking my clothes. It turns out that it was the fridge.

I think I've been eating too much salmon over Christmas. I've just tried to run up an escalator that was going down.

I asked the waitress for a quickie and she slapped me.

The old woman next to me said, "It's pronounced 'Quiche' dear."

Congratulations to my wife, who has managed a Culinary first.

She managed to set off the neighbours smoke detector from her own Kitchen.

There are two kinds of pedestrians: the quick and the dead.

32   I'll get my Jacket

A New York attorney representing a very wealthy art collector called and asked to speak to his client.

"Mr O'Toole, I have some good news and some bad news." He said.

"You know what Jack, I've had such a bad day, so let's have the good new first" He replied.

"Well" said The Solicitor. "I met with your Wife today and she informed me she only invested $5,000 on two very nice pictures that she thinks will bring in between $15 and $20 Million each, and I think she could be right."

The Collector replied enthusiastically "Holy cow, my wife is a brilliant businesswoman isn't she? You've just made my day. Now I think I can handle the bad news, tell me what it is."

The solicitor told him, "They are of you and your secretary!"

When my Grandad got ill the Doctor told us to rub lard onto his back. He went downhill pretty fast after that.

-

Have you had an accident in the last three years? They ask "you could claim compensation." They continue on. So I called claims direct, epecting to be passed on to a Solicitor, and a big cash payout. Only to be told that drinking 15 pints of real ale before sneezing and consequently following through was not considerdered an 'Accident'. It was not as though I did it on purpose.

I borrowed my wife's favourite audio book and deleted it by mistake...

I'm never gonna hear the end of it now

Gardening Rule: When weeding, the best way to make sure you are removing a weed and not a valuable plant is to pull on it. If it comes out of the ground easily, it is a valuable plant.

I used to be a freelance journalist but I wasn't very good.

Lance Is still in prison!

The easiest way to find something lost around the house is to buy a replacement.

Never take life seriously. Nobody gets out alive anyway.

Santa played a round of golf on Christmas day to relax and hit a birdie.... It was a partridge on a par 3.

Saw my mate riding in an old cart today so I shouted out "Hey Wayne".

I was walking home past the golf course and I realized I still had a fairway to go.

I hate Christmas shopping for the wife, I've just wasted two hours in a queue to discover Poundland don't do gift vouchers.

My wife said she would love a locket for Christmas.

I never even knew she had a sore throat

Went in a clothes shop in Birmingham and asked for a kipper tie. He asked how many sugars.

A guy walks into a bar with a monkey. The monkey grabbed some olives off the bar and ate them. Then he grabbed some sliced limes and ate them. He then jumped on to the pool table and grabbed one of the balls. To everyone's amazement, he stuck it in mouth and somehow swallowed it whole. The bartender looked at the guy and said "did you see what your monkey just did?"No what?" "He just ate the cue ball off my pool table... whole! "Yeah that doesn't surprise me," the guy he eats everything in sight, don't worry, I'll pay for the cue ball." The guy finished his drink, paid his bill paid for the stuff the monkey ate and left. Two weeks later the guy came back, and had his monkey with him. He ordered a drink and the monkey started running around the bar. The monkey found a maraschino cherry on the bar. He grabbed it stuck it up his arse, pulled it out then ate it. Then the monkey found a peanut, and again stuck it up his arse, pulled it out then ate it. The bartender asked "Did you see what your monkey just did?" "No, what?" replied the man. "Well, he stuck both a maraschino cherry and a peanut up his arse, pulled them out, and ate them!" "Yeah, that doesn't surprise me," replied the guy. "He will eat anything, but ever since he had to shit out that cue ball, he measures everything first".

I was a bit bored, so I opened the Celebration tub and put all the sweets indifferent wrappers. The wife was not amused she got all her snickers in a twix

Only when a mosquito lands on a man's balls, does he learn to solve a problem without violence.

So I went to Tokyo and got the words "jacuzzi" and "yakuza" mixed up. Now I'm in hot water with the Japanese mafia.

I wanted to buy an extra jar of pickled onions but my wife said no, that's shallot.

I got chatting with a girl in a bar last night. "Can I buy you a drink?" I asked.

"Don't you have a girlfriend?" she replied. "Guys like you always have girlfriends.

"No, sadly we broke up just over a month ago." I assured her.

"Oh I'm sorry to hear that." She said "Go on then I'll have a cider please."

After a few drinks and a few kissed we went back to her place and made passionate love Whilst putting my clothes back on she said to me. "So, you're good looking, a nice guy and amazing in bed. Can I ask you why on Earth you split with your girlfriend?'

I said "My wife found out!"

A man was marooned on a desert island. One day a beautiful woman arrives wearing a wet suit. "When did you last have a smoke?" she asked. "Five years ago" I replied. So, she gets a cigar out from her wet suit, hands it to him and he smokes it. She starts to unzip her wet suit a little further and asked "When was the last time you had a drink?" "Five years ago" he replied. So she produces a bottle of scotch from the wet suit. Hands it to him and he then had a drink. She unzipped her wet suit some more and asked "… and when was the last time you played around?" He looks at her in total amazement and says "Don't tell me you have a set of golf clubs in there!"

I wonder how many vampires have been run over by people who reverse their cars by just using their mirrors

I started my puncture repair business from a small Flat

When I get stressed I have a sandwich, a scone and a cup of tea out of a flask….
The doctor says I'm having picnic attacks

A praying ghost came to my door the other day.
It was a blessing in disguise.

Is it acceptable to dip bread into a curry?
Asking for my naan.

I'm returning this invisibility cloak I got for Christmas
I just can't see myself wearing it.

My wife has stood by me for 40 years.
We only have 1 chair.

Seems like only yesterday my brother rang to tell me I was an uncle to a baby boy, and that him and his wife were going to name him after me.
The years go by so quickly...
Afterme will be 21 next week!

Doctor to patient. "So, you are telling me you have a problem with one of your ears. Are you sure?"

Patient: "Yes doctor I am definite"

A mate of mine has just bought 10 barrels of air for his yacht. At first I thought it was odd but whatever floats your boat.

So if you tickle a man to death by accident...
Is it manslaughter?

I need to do something about my battery addiction.
Maybe start going to AAA meetings.

Just heard dentists are going on strike next week.
Brace yourselves

I asked a nurse where the Maternity ward was.
She said," Through the door marked Push, Push, Push"

We have a 99-year-old man in our darts team, so as a surprise we are going to fulfil his wish of spending his centenary birthday in the Caribbean.
He's going to be 100 in Haiti.

I wish that superglue remover I ordered comes soon.
Fingers crossed.

We had a famous singer deliver our supermarket groceries this week.
Sorry, I'm mistaken, it was a Morrison's Van

So I was in the pub when a guy comes in dressed as a referee, black shorts and top, whistle and flag.
I thought somethings going to kick off here!

I discovered that you can turn your ordinary sofa into a sofa bed simply by forgetting your wedding anniversary

---

I thought I'd found a mass snowman grave the other day.
Turned out it was just a field of carrots.

In 1964, Steve McQueen won a Superman lookalike contest because he was in the greatest cape.

Once upon a time in a Kingdom so far away, lived a King who ruled the kingdom in which all his people lived happily. This pleased the King, seeing his people in such a cheery manner. One day, things changed, a Big Bad Dragon came unto the kingdom, and started to burn and eat the population of the Kingdom so far way.

The King was desperate to save his people from the Big Bad Dragon. So desperate was he, that he offered a challenge to any knight who slayed the Big Bad Dragon and proved so by showing him its head, then that Knight would be offered the hand of his Beautiful Daughter the Princess and all the wealth that goes with it.

Now, the Big White Knight heard of this challenge, got on his Big White horse and took the long journey to the Kingdom so far away.

Upon his arrival at the Kingdom, he arranged a meeting with the King, and related the Challenge promoted by the King to any Knight. The King was impressed as the Big White Knight was the only challenger to the task.

And so The Big White Knight got on his Big White Horse and departed out from the Kingdom so far away to seek his destiny. On his journey he came across a village which looked poor, he asked for an ironmonger, who came forward to him.

"Mr Ironmonger I want you to make for me a sword and a spear strong enough to slay the Big Bad Dragon, which once done I can show the King from the Kingdom so far away. I will then take the hand of his Daughter, the Beautiful Princess. I will pay you handsomely should you accept." Said the Big White Knight sat on his Big White Horse. The task was taken up by the Ironmonger from the poor village, which was located outside of the Kingdom now not so far away.

A few days later the Big White Knight was told the Ironmonger had completed his task. He climbed on his Big White Horse and sought to see the Ironmonger located in the poor village.

"Ahh" said the Ironmonger "It is the Big White Knight sat on his Big White Horse!"

"Yes Mr Ironmonger tis I, and I have come to claim the task I set you." Said the Big White Knight, who then climbed down from the Big White Horse.

The Ironmonger showed the Big White Knight a marvelous Big Shiny sword and an equally magnificent bigger spear. The Big White Knight was pleased with what he saw, paid the Ironmonger well, and climbed back up onto his Big White Horse, making sure the Big Shiny and marvelous sword together with the equally Magnificent Bigger spear were secured to the Big White Horse. They then set off to the Kingdom now not so far away.

The Big White Knight on the Big White Horse found the Den of the Big Bad Dragon. He called into the Den with a Very Loud and Firm voice. "Big Bad Dragon it is I the Big White Knight and my Big White Horse, come out for I am tasked to slay you dead and return to the King so I can take the Hand of his beautiful Daughter the Princess.

The Big Bad Dragon came out of his den but before he could draw a Big Breath. The Big White Knight took hold of the Magnificent Big Spear and threw it at the Big Bad Dragon which struck at his throat and killed him stone dead. The Big White Knight got off the Big White Horse and took hold of the marvelous Big Shiny sword and chopped off the head of the now dead Big Bad dragon.

The Big White Knight put away both the Marvelous Big Shiny sword and the equally Magnificent Bigger spear onto the Big White Horse, tied up the head of the now Dead Big Bad Dragon, and dragged it to the Kingdom now not so far away.

The Big White Knight sat on His Big White Horse called out to the King. "Sire, I have slayed the Big Bad Dragon and have the evidence here."

The King look really impressed at what he saw. "Big White Knight sat on your Big White Horse, you have done well, all my Kingdom will be pleased. There was cheering all around, for the Big White Knight is now a Brave Big White Knight.

Sire, I have come to claim my prize can I have the hand of your Daughter, the Beautiful Princess and Marry her?"

I'll get my Jacket

The King replied…No!!

The End

I just found a half frozen tiny bird as I walked home, so I put it in my pocket to give it a chance of survival.

When I showed the wife, she told me how much she loved me for being so kind and sensitive, so I thought I'd try for a kiss & a cuddle, as she was in a good mood !!

She said "Please, not in front of the chilled wren".

Little Johnny's neighbor had a baby. But he was born without ears. Now, Johnny and his Mother went to visit the baby. Johnny was warned not to mention the baby's ears or he will be spanked. Johnny looked at the baby and said "What a lovely baby, nice hands and feet and lovely smooth skin. How is his eyesight?" He asked. The baby's Mother told him his eyes are perfect. "That's good" said Johnny, "Coz he would be buggered if he needed Glasses!"

Leading on from my interest in post-impressionist French artists , I discovered recently that a particular painter was the first to have two toilets in his house. His name?

Two Loos Lautrec

I called an old flame last night. Her Mum answered the phone and said, "She's gone out."

The football match between The Artists and The Sketchers ended in a draw.

Getting a bit worried about nan. She said she was having trouble doing a jigsaw of a tiger.

I said, "Nan, put the Frosties back in the box."

Chris Eubank has written a book about Ethics.

If it's successful, his next one will be about Kent.

I like to hit people on their knees to check their reflexes.

I just don't know why, but I get a kick out of it.

Police have just arrested me for stealing a sign that read, "& emergency". I had to tell them that I found it by Accident

---

Someone asked me if there was a B&Q in South Shields...I said no. but there are two D's in Dudley.

A cow just knocked on my front door trying to sell me double grazing.

My best friend loves 2 women. One makes incredible pancakes, The other writes beautiful poetry. Should he marry for batter or for verse?

A police officer turned up at my door this morning. "Do the letters TG mean anything to you?" He said. "No." I said.

"What about RP?" "No, means nothing to me." I said.

"How about AH?" He asked. "Look," I said "am I suspected of something?"

"No sir." He replied "These are just initial enquiries."

Just seen a great website on how to become a Ventriloquist; just go to

gubbillu, gubbillu, gubbillu, got. Com

I've just overheard my son telling a friend that he spent his dinner money on a skunk joint today. What's up with kids these days?
Beef, pork or lamb I can understand, but skunk?.

Watched a UB40 tribute act last night called WD40. They were a bit rusty at the start but got better as the night went on.

My Doctor told me," We have decided to keep the hip and replace the rest of you."

I've just bought a new sat-nav with a wild west theme, I tried it out for the first time today in South London. It gave me a route in Tooting in good time..

I found this on the menu at our local cafe - idemx rilgl.
I asked the waitress: "What is it?"
She said: "Mixed grill".

My right arm hurts like crazy, but only between 9 am & 11 am.
I've got ten-ish elbow.

King Arthur's troops usually wore very conservative clothes. Queen Guinevere demanded a more colorful dress code. This made them moody and blue so they refused to leave the round table.
The knights in white sat in.

Met a girl in a pub, she said "come outside and I'll show you a good time"
I went with her and she ran 100 metres in 9.98 seconds.

Every night lately, I dream of being in a hospital dressed in a gown and mask, delivering babies.
I must going through a midwife crisis.

A mate of mine bought a very cheap artificial leg; he's kicking himself now.

I am feeling really fit and healthy right now on my liquid diet, I am drinking plenty of different teas and have paid for this guy to come round teach me how to make it, this he does about me 3 times a week.
He's my personal strainer....

My calculator has suddenly stopped working.
Something doesn't add up here.

Whilst Alan Turing was decoding the Enigma machine, his sister Kay was busy making tea and sandwiches.

A man was seriously injured yesterday when his homemade bookcase fell on him.
He only has his shelf to blame.

Mariah Carey doesn't want turkey; all she wants for Christmas is stew!

As a Child - You're Grounded!
As an Adult - Your package will be delivered between 8am and 6pm.

Tonight we are going to the Amateur Ventriloquist Society's Christmas Gall.

Interviewer "We are looking for a responsible person for this job."

Candidate: "That's me. Wherever I have worked and something goes wrong. They said I was responsible."

A Pathologist is examining the corpse of unidentified murdered woman. Pointing to the many odd spiraling marks on her chest he turned to the two awaiting detectives, "This woman was a children's coach driver - Note how the Wheals On the Bust Go Round and Round?"

If three dinosaurs sing "Wuthering Heights", is it a Brontechorus

---

Putting Lentils in your pocket, means you've always got your fingers on the pulse

-At my nativity play none of the kids were allowed to be animals. We all had to be trees or hills. Apparently children were meant to be scene and not herd.

A young Irish man called Paddy wanted to buy a Christmas present for his new girlfriend. They hadn't been seeing each other for very long and she lived in Donegal and he lived in Kerry . Paddy consulted with his sister and decided, after careful consideration, that a pair of good quality gloves would strike the right note... not too romantic and not too personal. Off he went with his sister to Marks and Spencer's and they selected a dainty pair of fur lined quality leather gloves. His sister bought a pair of sexy knickers for herself at the same time. Marks and Spencer's had a free gift wrap offer but the assistant mixed up the two items, the sister got the gloves and Paddy unknowingly got the knickers. Good old Paddy sent off his gift wrapped present in a parcel with the following letter.

Dear Maggie

I chose these because I've noticed that you are not wearing any when we go out in the evenings. If it had not been for my sister I would have chosen the long ones with buttons, but she wears shorter ones (which are easier to remove). These are a very delicate shade, but the lady I bought them from showed me the pair she had been wearing for the past three weeks and I hardly noticed any marks. I had her try yours on for me and she looked really smart in them even though they were a little bit tight on her. She also said that they rub against her ring which helps keep it clean. In fact, she hasn't needed to wash it since she began wearing them.

I wish I was there to put them on for you the first time, as no doubt many other hands will touch them before I have a chance to see you again.

When you take them off remember to blow into them a little bit because they will be naturally a little damp from wearing.

Just imagine how many times my lips will kiss them during the coming year.

I hope you will wear them for me on our next date.

All my love,

Patrick

P.S. My mum tells me that the latest style is to wear them folded down with a little bit of fur showing

My friends clubbed together and bought me a caravan as a birthday gift for my love of travel, I don't want to sound ungrateful but does anyone want 6 camels?

I bought myself a first aid kit yesterday.
I thought I'd treat myself

A lost James Stewart film has been discovered about a poor man who only ever owned a single coat.
"It's A One Duffle Life"

A German bloke I know said
"I can do a brilliant impersonation of a sausage"
I said "Go on then, do your wurst"

My Yoga instructor was drunk today, put me in a very awkward position.

You could hear a pin drop at work today....
...not good when you work in a hand grenade factory.

.

Me: My wife and I are keen on rambling.
Friend: Fell walking?
Me: Yes, but she's fine now.

I've just started up a company manufacturing over-sized sinks and baths..

Does anyone on here mind if I give them a massive plug?

When I was young, I decided to go to Medical School. At the entrance exam, We were asked to arrange the letters PNEIS. and form the name of an important which is important when erect. Those who answered SPINE are now Doctors, while the rest are on Facebook.

Our local dentist is doing half price teeth cleaning today, it's plaque Friday!

I bought a book today on how to cure Kleptomania. Well... I say a bought it...

Just arrived for my speed awareness course an hour early.

I owed a lot of money to our local herbalist
He sent the bay leafs round.

There's this guy in our town centre who's always trying to cadge money off passers-by, but argues with everybody - including those that give him cash

He begs to differ.

The old Saxon King Alfred was known for burning the cakes. But he was always very forgetful when he was cleaning the fire place.

His wife was very often heard shouting at him, "Alfred, the Grate.

Patient: "Will I be OK Doc?"

Doctor: "I doubt it, Murcury in in Uranus just now"

Patient: "I don't do that Astrology stuff."

Doctor: "Me neither, my thermometer just broke!"

My Missus and three of her pals squeezed into my car after weight watchers. I muttered "Fat Cows" The missus snapped "What was that?" I replied "You Herd"

A Man applies for a job with the Scottish Police force. The Chief inspector says "These are the best qualifications I have ever seen. Just one test before we can hire you. Take this gun and go and shoot Paedofile, priests, Celtic Supporters and a rabbit."

The guy replies, "Why the Rabbit?

Chief Inspector says. "Good answer can you start on Monday?"

A thief broke into the local police station and stole their toilet, after an intense investigation the police have nothing to go on!!!

I've just bought a non- stick frying pan and some super glue. It should be interesting.

Parked outside my favourite restaurant and got a ticket.

Fined dining!

My grandmother just reached 105.

That's the last time I get in the car with her when she's late for bingo...

I only got my wife a large pack of playing cards for her birthday. Now she's trying to make a big deal of it.

I get stressed in my job parking aircraft in buildings.

I've been sent on a hangar management course

Hank Marvin is surprisingly well known for someone who has spent most of his life in the shadows.

A woman and child were in the doctors waiting for a check-up the doctor examines the baby and declares that he is under weight, he asks if the baby is bottle fed or breast fed? the woman says breast fed, he orders the woman to strip down to the waist. After squeezing her breasts and tweaking her nipples he says to the woman that the problem is you have no milk, she says I'm the grandmother but I'm glad I came.

My grandfather's a little forgetful, but he likes to give me advice. One day he took me aside and left me there.

I went to a fancy dress party dressed as a tea bag.

Got mugged on my way home!

Cher is making appearances with one of her impersonators.

They're billed as Cher and Cher Alike.

Saw a old policeman's uniform in a charity shop.

I thought 'That fits the bill'.

I recently bought an old painting by a renowned artist. When I picked it up it wasn't as heavy as I thought. I was going to tell you all about it but my Monet's too light too mention.

The inventor of the sponge was from Athens.

His name was Absorber the Greek.

Just found out my dad was a mime artist. He kept that quiet.

My wife's obsession with collecting colanders has put a real strain on our relationship.

I think the girl at the Airlines check-in just threatened me.

She looked me dead in the eye and said, "Window or aisle?"

I laughed in her face and replied, "Window or you'll what?

Had a operation on my funny bone once

I was in stitches for two weeks.

Just been to the shop when a lion walked in and got on the escalator.

You should have seen the uproar.

"This next song is by a group called The Bailiffs;

"Take it away boys"

Charles Dickens walks into a pub.

The barman says to him "All right Sir?"

"Not really," says Dickens, "I can't think of a name for the main character in one of my books. Give me a Martini."

The barman said," Olive or twist?"

Bought the wife some crotch less knickers today. Not for any sexual reason, more like health and safety.

She can now grip her broomstick better!

GCSE History Exam.

Name 3 famous characters associated with cakes.

Answer - Alfred the Great, Marie Antoinette and Mr Kipling.

A burglar has been caught breaking into the local library….I hope they throw the book at him

---

I met a bloke recently who told me that he was a lollipop man at Jellystone Park, I told him that I used to be a lollipop man at Hundred Acre Wood.

He said we all have our bears to cross

Ignore the Best Before date on baked beans.

They are pretty much the worst thing you can eat before going on a date.

So I got chased for ages the other day by a man trying to steal my wallet.

I thought to myself, "He's giving me a good run for my mon

Banks should do a better job at keeping their ATMs filled.

That's the 5th one I've been to today that's said "Insufficient funds!

I gave my friend an apple, and he told me he preferred pears.

So I gave him another apple.

Bit cold this morning, when I opened our curtains I thought I saw David Jason

But it was only a touch of frost.

"I'd like a pair of boots that come bit above the knees."

"Thighs?"

"Thix or maybe a theven."

For my birthday, I was given a surprise trip to a very big orchard. Stood around amazed at the hundreds of trees. It was not the Apple Watch I was expecting!

I was in the bank today and the girl behind the counter kept whistling Down town.

I thought what a peculiar clerk

I'm so important now, I've decided to pay for a police escort.

It's a 1972 model, only 88,000 miles on the clock.

A man was leaving a cafe with his morning coffee when he noticed a most unusual funeral procession approaching the nearby cemetery. A long black hearse was followed by a second-long black hearse about 20 yards behind the first.

Behind the second hearse was a solitary man walking a pit-bull on a leash. Behind him was a queue of 200 men walking in single file.

The man couldn't stand the curiosity. He respectfully approached the man walking the dog.

"I am so sorry for your loss, and I know now is a bad time to disturb you, but I've never seen a funeral like this with so many of you walking in single file. Whose funeral is it?"

The man replied, "Well, the first hearse is for my wife."

"What happened to her?"

The man replied, "My dog attacked and killed her."

He inquired further, "Well, who is in the second hearse?"

The man answered, "My mother-in-law. She was trying to help my wife when the dog turned on her."

A poignant and thoughtful moment of silence passes between the two men.

" Can I borrow the dog?"

" Join the queue."

One of the Russian acrobats in our human pyramid has been deported.

We don't have Oleg to stand on

I hated playing the Triangle in the school orchestra.

It was just one ting after another.

Sky have won the rights to the World Origami Championship.

Unfortunately, it's only on paper view.

This bloke asked me if I'd any idea where he could get a new wig from?

I said not off the top of my head.

So my girlfriend dumped me she was sick of my shampoo obsession

Shame, she was Head and Shoulders above the rest.

I hear that Julius Caesar was a very agreeable chap.

"I came I saw I concurred"

Someone said his mate came off his motorbike yesterday, he's got brain damage two broken arms and blind in one eye. I said blimey no wonder he came off his bike.

Olav the Viking in a Supermarket, when he comes across an old lady in a wheel chair almost in Tears.

"What's the matter?" asked Olav.

"Oh" sobs the old lady. "I want to look at the puddings but, as you can see they are three steps down to the chiller cabinet"

"No problem" said Olav and picked up the old lady onto his back. "I'll take you"

Olav strolls through the cabinets with the old lady, she selects seveal puddings and places them in the basket he is carrying. At the other end the old lady's husband is waiting for her with the wheelchair.

"I'd really like to thank you" says the old lady as Olav placed her back into the Wheelchair. "But I don't even know who you are?"

Olav just waves and departs the area.

"I've been worrying about you" says the old ladies husband. "What have you been doing?" he asked.

She replied "I've been through the desserts with a Norse with no name!"

My presentation on the origins of cotton turned into a bit of a disaster:

I just lost my thread!

I've just seen two police officers lying next to a seesaw.

They must have been tipped off

They have just discovered a fossil of a prehistoric monster in Haworth.

They believe it to be a Brontesaurus

"Why are those rabbits, guinea pigs & white mice bobbing about in the river?"

"It's the pet shop buoys"

My wife asked for some peace and quiet whilst she was cooking.

So I took the battery out of the smoke alarm.

I went into the local shop and asked if they had seen a seaman with one arm and one leg.

They said "Sorry we're wholesalers".

Apparently it's no longer politically-correct to direct a joke at any racial or ethnic minority, so here goes:

An Englishman, a Scotsman, an Irishman, a Welshman, a Gurkha, a Latvian, a Turk, an Aussie, two Kiwis, a German, an American, a South African, a Cypriot, an Egyptian, a Japanese, a Mexican, a Spaniard, a Russian, a Pole, a Lithuanian, a Swede, a Finn, an Israeli, a Dane, a Romanian, a Bulgarian, a Serb, a Swiss, a Greek, a Singaporean, an Italian, a Norwegian, a Libyan, a Muslim, a Hindu, a Buddhist and an Ethiopian went to a night club.

The bouncer said, "Sorry, I can't let you in without a Thai.

A 5 year old granddaughter is taken to school daily by her grandfather.

When he had a bad cold his wife took the grandchild.

That night she told her parents that the ride to school with granny was very different!!

"What made it different?" asked her parents.

"Today on the way to school Gran and I didn't see a single tosser, blind bastard, dick-head, Asian pr..k, or wanker anywhere!"

The police knocked on my door last night and said 'Can we have a quick word?'

I said, 'Sure, Velocity'

So I went into my local printers this morning and said, "I need a 6 foot A, a 6 foot S and a 6 foot K, and I need them by tomorrow".

He said, "I'll see what I can do but it's a big ask..."

Went to a classic car show yesterday.

Saw a car that had two pints of milk , a block cheese , 6 eggs and half a pound of butter on the back seat.

It was a Lada

I've just seen a load of people raiding a music shop stealing violins and trumpets. So I decided to step in... I'm taking a stand.

Apparently my blind date tonight is around 6 feet 6 inches tall.

I can't wait two metre.

A man goes to the doctor with hearing problems.

"Can you describe the symptoms to me?" asked the doctor.

"Yes. Homer is a fat, lazy and yellow and Marge is a skinny bird with big blue hair.

Warnings are so stupid. Like on this deodorant: 'Avoid contact with eyes' Too late, I've already seen it

---

My friend David lost his ID.

I just call him Dav now

I used to go out with a girl who was a gym instructor.

Didn't work out.

Just heard that the man who stole my personal and private diary has died.

My thoughts are with his family

I married a Swedish military woman. I now have my own Swiss army wife

I went to church today and the vicar called me over and asked not swear in front of his wife.

I honestly didn't realize it was her turn.

Went for a walk past a farm with my new girlfriend and we saw dogs mating.

She said: "How does the male know when the female is ready for sex?"

I replied: "He can smell she is ready. That's how nature works."

We then walked past a sheep field and the ram was mating the ewe.

Again my girlfriend asked: "How does the ram know when the ewe is ready for sex?"

I replied: "It's nature. He can smell she is ready."

We then went past another pasture and the bull was mating with the cow.

My girlfriend said: "This is odd. They are really going at it. Surely the bull can't smell when she is ready?"

I said: "Oh, yes; it's nature. All animals can smell when the female is ready for sex."

Anyway, after the walk, I dropped her at home and kissed her goodbye.

She said: "Take care and get yourself tested for Covid-19."

A matelot was driving down the M1 Motorway with his lovely blonde girlfriend when she piped up;

"I think those people in the car next to us are from Wales".

"Why do you think that?" he said.

"Well, the kids are writing on the window and it says:

"stit ruoy su wohs".

I went into the sweet shop this morning and asked for a Boost, a Twirl and a Topic.

The shopkeeper said, "You look great", then spun round and said, "What's your view on Global Warming?

I'm surrounded by vegetables in jars. It's like Piccalilli circus in here

---

My mate went to a concert in the Far East.

I asked: "Singapore?"

He said: "Yes, and the musicians were rubbish too

Just done a Speed Awareness course, 3 hours long… blimey that went quickly.

Because I've never sketched a scrabble set before, I've asked loads of people for advice.

So far I've drawn a blank.

We called our latest child Ivy. We'd run out of names and started using Roman Numerals.

Mike invited his mother over for dinner. During the course of the meal, Mike's mother couldn't help but notice how beautiful Mike's roommate Jennifer was.

Mike's mom had long been suspicious of the 'platonic' relationship between Mike and Jennifer, and this had only made her more curious.

Over the course of the evening, while watching the two interact, she started to wonder if there was more between Mike and Jennifer than met the eye.

Reading his mom's thoughts, Mike volunteered, "I know what you must be thinking, but I assure you Jennifer and I are just roommates."

About a week later, Jennifer came to Mike saying, "Ever since your mother came to dinner, I've been unable to find that beautiful silver gravy ladle. You don't suppose she took it, do you?"

Mike said, "Well, I doubt it, but I'll send her an e-mail just to be sure." So he sat down and sent her a message:

"Dear Mom,

I'm not saying that you did take the gravy ladle from the house, I'm not saying that you did not take the gravy ladle. But the fact remains that it has been missing ever since you were here for dinner.

Love, Mike"

Several days later, Mike received an email back from his mother that read:

"Dear Son,

I'm not saying that you do sleep with Jennifer, I'm not saying that you do not sleep with Jennifer. But the fact remains that if Jennifer was sleeping in her own bed, she would have found the gravy ladle by now.

Love, Mom"

Two men wearing baklava's just ambushed me with a cake.

I'm having trouble sleeping so I bought a CD, "Sounds of the Ocean". I put it on and there's nothing on it! So I took it back to the shop and the man said "Well, the tides out isn't it"

So my first flat was so close to Heathrow airport, that every time I went to the kitchen to make a sandwich, a stewardess told me to get back to my seat!

Accordian to a recent survey, replacing words with a musical instrument in a sentence often goes undetected.

It's hard to say what my girlfriend does for a living

She sells seashells on the seashore

Fred got a job as a Handy Man. The first day they asked him to mend the door.

"Sorry", He said, "I don't do carpentry'

"We Well", they said, "Can you dig the Garden?"

"No sorry", he said, "I've got a bad back"

So they said, "What's handy about you?"

"I only live round the corner.

I'll get my Jacket

The police knocked on my door last night and said 'Can we have a quick word?'

I said, 'Sure, Velocity'

So I went into my local printers this morning and said, "I need a 6 foot A, a 6 foot S and a 6 foot K, and I need them by tomorrow".

He said, "I'll see what I can do but it's a big ask..."

Went to a classic car show yesterday.

Saw a car that had two pints of milk , a block cheese , 6 eggs and half a pound of butter on the back seat.

It was a Lada

I've just seen a load of people raiding a music shop stealing violins and trumpets. So I decided to step in... I'm taking a stand.

Apparently my blind date tonight is around 6 feet 6 inches tall.

I can't wait two metre.

A man goes to the doctor with hearing problems.

"Can you describe the symptoms to me?" asked the doctor.

"Yes. Homer is a fat, lazy and yellow and Marge is a skinny bird with big blue hair."

....

I called Gamblers Anonymous to ask what time I should be there.

They said ten to one.

....

My Wife says she is leaving me because of my obsession with Sylvester Stallone movies!

To be honest though, things have been Rocky for a while.

....

This bloke said to me: 'I'm going to attack you with the neck of a guitar.'

I said: 'Is that a fret?

....

I was hit by a bottle of Omega 3 tablets,

Luckily my wounds are

'Super Fish Oil'

....

I used to work in a Fish & Chip restaurant, but I didn't like it, so I got a job in a cinema, as a commissionaire.

For me it was out of the frying pan in to the foyer.

....

I went to the doctors about my lack of hearing.

He gave me some drops, and told me to put two in my beers every day.

I have been doing it for 2 weeks now, and it hasn't made a bit of difference

....

Louis XIV was known as the Sun King.

Because he never reigned when it poured.

....

I've started naming my friends after high Street stores.

You're next.

....

I was just stood next to someone shouting really loudly for their dog Snowy and now I've got Tintinitis.

....

Looking at a top in a shop today, I looked the shop assistant and she said, 'You can try it on if you like'.

I said 'OK, what are you doing this weekend?'

....

I didn't get the job hypnotizing chickens.

I failed the hen trance exam.

....

Went out for dinner last night and ordered fish in a herb sauce.

It tasted weird and I was going to complain but I didn't know if it was the thyme or the plaice.

....

The last three surviving Wildebeest have just died! Well, that's the end of the gnus, here's the weather forecast.

....

I bought a new sofa from DFS today.

The assistant told me, it will seat six people without a problem.

Where the heck am I going to find 6 people without a problem?

....

I left my last girlfriend because she wouldn't stop counting.

I often wonder what she's up to now

....

Wife: "For Pete's sake, I'm getting sick and tired of you accusing me of cheating on you!"

Husband: "Who's Pete?"

....

Walking home from the pub late last night, I turned the corner and there was an Apple Turnover in the middle of the road.

The next one had a rhubarb crumble in the middle of the road and when I turned into my road there was a large trifle.

I thought, the Streets are strangely deserted tonight.

....

Wife. "I have blisters on my hands from the broom".

Me. "Take the car next time".

....

Got the sack this morning, just because I turned up in a big floppy hat with a feather in it, knee length leather boots and a Ruff

Apparently the Boss didn't like my Cavalier Attitude

....

I love my electric blanket!

I'm never going back to an acoustic one.

....

Just found out that the French man who I thought was my dad was not my dad after all.

He was my faux pa.

I was sacked from my job at the local DIY store for stealing paint.

I loved that job so I'm leaving with mixed emulsions.

....

My Nail Salon assistant, Tracy, has gone missing.

It's not easy to varnish without Trace.

....

I bought a chess set from a pal yesterday...

I asked him, "Is it alright if i pay by cheque mate?"

....

Which famous Roman suffered from hay fever?

Julius Sneezer.

....

I was staring at a bit of pasta stuck to the ceiling wondering how it got up there.

Then the penne dropped...

....

Sad to report that the talks about the merger of the AA and the RAC have broken down.

....

The wife crashed the car into some bloke yesterday. She told the police he'd been on his mobile and drinking beer.

The police said he could do what he wanted in his conservatory.

....
.

Disappointed to be charged £15.99 for a plate of calamari this evening.

I expected it would just be a couple of squid.

....

Entered a cooking competition but used dogfood by mistake.

Needless to say I didn't win a lot.

....

I got invited to a party and was told to dress to kill. Apparently a turban, beard and a backpack wasn't what they had in mind.

Paddy says to Mick, "Christmas is on Friday this year". Mick said, "Let's hope it's not the 13th then."

A lad comes home from school and excitedly tells his dad that he had a part in the school play and he was playing a man who had been married for 25 years. The dad says, "Never mind son, maybe next year you'll get a speaking part."

After years of research, scientists have discovered what makes women happy. Waste of money if you ask me as we all know the answer already.... Nothing.

Did you hear about the fat, alcoholic transvestite? All he wanted to do was eat, drink and be Mary

The inventor of the throat lozenge died, there was no Coffin at his funeral

So I called "The Subtraction Café" and asked to book a table.

They said they only do takeaways.

....

Scottish water has been awarded the contract to flush all the pipes around Buckingham Palace this week. A Scottish Water spokesperson said

We are delighted and honoured to be part of The Queens chlorination

....
.

I've just found 5 Mars bars, 3 Snickers, a Flake and a packet of M&M's.

I'm starting to think; I'm not cut out to be a Bounty hunter.

....

I was working in Subway recently, when Elton John came in and asked for a ham salad sandwich.

'Lettuce?' I asked.

'No, I'm a rocket man'

....

My wife tells me I'm a terrible Parker.

She also reckons that my Lady Penelope impression is even worse.

....

Entered a cooking competition but used dogfood by mistake.

Needless to say I didn't win a lot.

....

Ever felt the need to make a car dealer feel uncomfortable?

Just open the boot of the car, climb inside, shut the lid and ask him if he can hear screaming.

....

I have been tracing my family tree and found my great Grandfather used to be the foreman in a napkin factory in Russia.

He was the leader of the Serviette Union.

....

Reports are coming in of a large Yorkshire city disappearing overnight! Police are desperately looking for Leeds

Problem with loose keys on your computer keyboard?

Fix them with superglue, but take care nottttttttttttttttttttttttttttttttttttttttttttttttttttt

....

The doctor has given me some cream for my excessive gloating - I can't wait to get home and rub it in.

Managed to get myself a job in the travelling Circus as a contortionist. Mind you I had to bend over backwards to get through the interview

....

BREAKING: An earthquake hit near a biscuit factory in the North of England last night...

It measured 2.8 on the Rich Tea scale!

....
.

Wonderful news I've just got a job as a steamroller driver.

I'm flat out at the minute

....
.

Just found out I was adopted as a kid by a man called Daz.

He's my Non Biological father

....

I phoned up the TV shopping channel and they said "Hello, can I help you?".

I said "No thanks, I'm just looking"

....

I knew a farmer who fed his pregnant pig marmite.

Last week she had 12 twiglets

....

We were arguing all day about what you call a medieval soldier.

But then it got late, so we called it a knight.

....

As I was climbing into the new bed I bought us last night, my wife snarled at me and turned the other way.

I think she's jealous that I got the top bunk.

If you're trying to fit a square peg in a round hole, maybe you shouldn't be messing around in the Early Learning Centre.

....

I was at the zoo today and i saw a large bird standing on 1 leg singing opera.

I said to the warden, "That's amazing".

He said, "Yes, it's Placido Flamingo.

....

Return of the Jedi is not possible without the Receipt of the Jedi.

....
.

Little known fact.

In Iran everyone is afraid of spiders, but in Iraq, no phobia.

....

I think the ghost of Cilla Black is singing in my Stationery Warehouse.

At night I can hear "Supplies Supplies!"

I've just finished reading Great Expectations

It wasn't as good as I thought it was going to be.

....

My Boss told me that if I can get through today without mentioning biscuits he will give me £100.

Nice…

....

I've just heard that what my grandfather did in the war was very hush hush.

He worked in the library

....

It was chaos lining up at the world yodeling contest last week until a steward yelled,

"EVERYONE FORM AN ORDERLY ORDELY ORDERLY ORDERLY ORDERLY ORDERLY QUEUUUUUUUUE!!!"

....

I was in a Cafe happily dipping my biscuits in other people's tea and they called the police... Apparently I was Dunkin' disorderly

....

Back in the 1970's our Auntie got a black and white dog as she thought the license would be cheaper"

....

My car was making a horrible knocking noise so I got out to have a look.

It turned out I'd run over a Jehovah's Witness.

....

I've just been caught doing 50mph through the village whilst out on my Horse.

I've got to take a Steed awareness course!!

....

In the pub last night, a woman was saying her calves looked sexy in high heels.

I've reported her to the RSPCA.

....

The inventor of the Taser passed away.

All his friends were stunned.

....

I bought a packet of Powered Water but it didn't say what to mix it with

....

Just discovered Alfie Boe's brother Harry manufactures sweets

....

I saw a spin-off of Man About the House set in 1700's where the bloke hated working at the cotton factory.

Georgian Mill Dread

....

Our local cheap supermarket has a new Humpty Dumpty toy in stock.

It's brilliant and comes with Aldi Kings Horses and Aldi Kings Men!

....

So I went to a fancy dress party last week, dressed as a screwdriver. It turned a few heads…

....

My boss said to me "Why do you come out in a rash when I give you your wages?"

I said "It's because I'm allergic to peanuts!"

....

My wife left me because of my obsession with the Police force. My four sons Victor Oscar, Mike and Charlie have been very supportive. However, my two eldest children Romeo and Juliet won't talk to me about it.

....

I like to pretend I'm Les Dennis by putting my arm around a stranger at Waterloo Station and looking up at the departure board.

....

I've been watching the curling and the men's and ladies' bob this morning.

It wasn't the Olympics I was waiting for a haircut.

....

Last week I shortened the rope that's tied to the bucket which we use to get our water...It didn't go down well..

I once had a girlfriend called Peg....We met online.

Well, I say girlfriend...I just used to hang out with her

⋯⋯⋯⋯⋯⋯⋯⋯⋯⋯⋯⋯⋯⋯⋯⋯⋯⋯⋯⋯⋯⋯⋯⋯⋯⋯⋯

One of my uncle's favourite quotes was "None shall pass".

Nice guy, terrible Driving Examiner.

⋯⋯⋯⋯⋯⋯⋯⋯⋯⋯⋯⋯⋯⋯⋯⋯⋯⋯⋯⋯⋯⋯⋯⋯⋯⋯⋯

I've just moved into a new flat directly above a police station.

Does that mean I'm above the law now

⋯⋯⋯⋯⋯⋯⋯⋯⋯⋯⋯⋯⋯⋯⋯⋯⋯⋯⋯⋯⋯⋯⋯⋯⋯⋯⋯

I asked the guy at the sweet shop why I could hear crying coming from one of the shelves...

He said "That's a sensitive Topic"

⋯⋯⋯⋯⋯⋯⋯⋯⋯⋯⋯⋯⋯⋯⋯⋯⋯⋯⋯⋯⋯⋯⋯⋯⋯⋯⋯

Shakespeare wrote all of his play's in pencil, but took ages to decide what degree of pencil hardness to use .

Husband's Text Message to wife:

Honey, I got hit by a car outside the office.

Paula brought me to the Hospital. Doctors presently doing tests and taking X-rays.

Severe blow to my head but not likely to have any lasting effects. Wound required 19 stitches.

I have three broken ribs, a broken arm and compound fracture in the left leg. Amputation of the right foot is a possibility. Love you.

Wife's Response:

Who's Paula?

....

"Holmes's, why is your front door painted yellow?"

"Lemon entry my dear Watson! "

....
.

Diana Ross oiled her bike and came out in a terrible rash.

Apparently she had a chain reaction.

....

Mick Hucknall of Simply Red goes to the physio and says "My knee is so sore".

The physio asks "How tight is it?"

And he says, "My knee's too tight to mention".

....

The swordfish has no natural predators, the Penfish, which is supposed to be even mightier.

....

It was so windy on my walk home from the Gym last night, I was blown into a Chip Shop

My girlfriend phoned me and said, "I've got something to tell you, but it's hard to say."

So I said nervously, "Go on..."

She said...

"Ken Dodd's Dad's dog's dead."

....

My daughter has just told me she wants to drive a steamroller when she's older.

I said," Sure, I won't stand in your way"

A bloke at the races came over and whispered: "Do you want the winner of the next race?".

I said: "No thanks, I've only got a small garden".

Our dog plays the cello very badly.

In fact, his Bach is worse than his bite!

When I lived in London I taught my dog to play the trumpet on the underground!. He went from Barking to Tooting in 10 minutes.

....

How many Countdown contestants does it take to change a BLIHBULGT?

....

For all those who believe in psychokinesis, please raise my right hand.

....

Is it true that an apple a day keeps the doctor away or is it just one of Granny's myths?

....

So when James Bond is abroad, is he known as +4407?

....

I just read a book entitled, "100 things to do before you die"

I was quite surprised to see that "shout for help" wasn't in there!

....

It's a lovely crisp morning,

I've had three bags already.

....

My house security camera caught a guy, completely naked, stealing an apple from my tree.

Didn't know him from Adam.

....

My fishmonger has smelly breath - he suffers from Halibutosis.

....

I had to thank my Scottish builder for resurfacing my drive.

Ta Mac!

....

I always wanted to be a monk..

But I didn't get the chants…

....

I find it hard to believe that my rock and roll hero had his detractors.

I'll be sure to watch the new documentary - Buddy Holly and the critics.

....

I've written a book about the history of WD-40..

You can find it in the library under non friction section.

....

Police have confirmed the man who tragically fell from the 18th floor Nightclub was not a Bouncer

....

I'm not saying it rough out there yesterday but one of my hens just laid the same egg 3 times.

....

Due to the current economic crisis, Greece is cancelling all production of humus and Taramasalata.

It's a double dip recession.

....

I can't stand those interfering people who bang on your door and tell you how you need to be 'saved' or you will 'burn'..

Pesky firemen.

....

I've asked my wife to polish my medieval battle uniform when for I go to the reenactment practice tomorrow evening.

She always said she wanted a night in, shining armour

....

I was terrible at spelling when I was in school.

I was brilliant at Jografy though

....
.

I used to sell ice cream during the interval at our local cinema.

When I got married I walked down the aisle backwards.

I stayed in a posh hotel in London recently and it had a golf course on the roof.

Who ever thought that one day I'd be Putting on the Ritz.

....

A young lady walks into a supermarket. On her way around the aisles she sees a chap who'd had his wicked way with her the previous evening after they had met at a club.

He was stacking washing powder boxes on the shelves. "You lying bastard!" she shouts. "Last night you told me you were a stunt pilot!"

"No" he replied "I told you I was a member of the Ariel display team."

....

I asked my neighbour why he wears the same high-visibility jacket to work every day.

He said it's his favourite, he wouldn't be seen without it.

....

When my wife is feeling Sad & Blue, I let her colour in my tattoos. She likes a shoulder to Crayon

....

My mate's had amnesia for as long as he can remember.

....

I thought I heard 'Tubular Bells' on Our Farm last winter.

It was coming from my cold field

I was going to hire a landscape gardener but he said he couldn't help me as my garden was portrait.

....

I've just successfully bred a cross between a crocodile and a homing pigeon.

I bet that'll come back to bite me.

....

Did you know nobody lives in Greenwich permanently,

They're just staying there in the meantime.

....

There is a free-view channel called yesterday+1.... Isn't that today?

....

Bouncer at a nightclub said to me

"Sorry, you can't come in, you've had a few too many"

I said "I haven't had one drink yet!"

He said "Not drinks, Birthdays"

She said she couldn't sleep with the light on.

I told her to go and never darken my lighthouse again.

....

Although I was fired from the Foreign Currency Bureau for being lazy, if I had my time again I still wouldn't change a thing.

....

Never invite John Milton around for a game of Monopoly.

Every time we do, there is a pair of dice lost.

....

Dear Optimist, Pessimist, and Realist,

While you were busy arguing over the glass of water… I drank it

Sincerely,

The opportunist

....

I had a fear of chestnut trees but now I've conkered it

I saw a bloke walking down the road near the Local Hospital with a sign under his arm that read,

"& Emergency"...

I asked, "Where did you get that from mate?

He said, "I found it by Accident"..

Having regained consciousness after a car accident the Doctor is trying to convince me that I am actually a Swedish guy and I have lost my memory.

Yeah right.. ...does he think I was Bjorn yesterday

Breaking news -a strange animal described as a cross between an Australian semi aquatic mammal and an overweight moggy was seen at a local lake attacking and eating several mallards.

Police are looking for a duck filled fatty puss

My driving instructor is doing my head in. He only let's me take the wheel on straight roads and when we get near corners he makes us swap positions.

Honestly he's driving me round the bend.

I met a Flat Earth Society member yesterday

He'd just came back from a trip to the

Arctic Square

....

I'll never forget my Grandad coming home from the war with one leg. We never did find out who it belonged to

....

So I gave my nephew six pieces of cardboard for His birthday.

He asked: "What's this?"

I replied: "It's an ex box…"

....

My dad used to say "Cleanliness is next to godliness".

We never did find the missing pages from his dictionary.

....

I guessed orange, but it was chocolate; I guessed toffee, but it was peanut; I guessed strawberry, but it was coffee.

I was wrong on so many Revels

....

The man who invented the snooze button died.

His funeral is at 10am and then 8 minutes later.

....

Bloke waiting on a bone marrow transplant hears there is a donor called Diego in Argentina.

The operation goes ahead and is successful so the bloke decides to write to him to thank him.

He starts the letter, "Dear Diego marrow donor"

....
.

I told my boss that 3 companies were after me, so I needed a large pay rise.

He asked,"Which companies?"

Gas Water and Electricity.

....

A restaurant that kept serving soggy rice has been given a restraining order.

....

I have this compulsion to keep standing up and shouting,

"BROCCOLI AND CAULIFLOWER "

I think I may have Florettes

....

Honestly!

I do one little Google search and now all the adverts on my timeline are for Arsenic and Cyanide

....

Police are looking for the gang who got away in a van after they robbed a paper mill in Bristol.

It's believed that they took the A4.

....

Wherever you go to in Hawaii you'll always hear the song "Shout" - in hotels, restaurants and airports.

It's because they honour Lulu.

Why do seagulls fly over the ocean?

Because if they flew over the bay, we'd call them bagels.

My friend was arrested for his beliefs.

He believed the night watchman was asleep, but wasn't!

The hardest part about making skimmed milk, is throwing the cow across the lake.

Just came home and told my wife about a funny encounter I had this morning helping a man in a black robe with a scythe clear the ice off his car.

She seems to think I was de-icing with death.

I just put up a high voltage electric fence around my house.

My neighbour is dead against it.

I saw my doctor today, he said "What's the problem?"

I said "I keep feeling like I'm an ocean"

He said, "Can you be more pacific?"

....

My wife is getting treatment for her irrational fear of sea birds but she's not getting any better.

In fact, she's taken a tern for the worse…

....

Ever since having a bullet removed from my thigh I've had shooting pains in my leg.

....

Got a pair of boxers with the London Underground map on for Christmas.

Already had to change twice.

....

I told my daughter that I saw a deer on the way to work this morning.

She asked, "How did you know it was on its way to work?"

....

I accidentally just knocked someone over in Dominos Pizza.

Well, I say one...

....

And God promised men that good and obedient wives would be found in all corners of the World. He then made the World round. He laughed and laughed and laughed

....

My dog kept chasing people on a bike. So we took his bike off him.

Then he just sat in the garden and barked all day.

So we gave him his bike back.

Because his bark was worse than his bike....

....

I see that Brazilian singer/actress has moved her fruit basket to the porch.

Carmen Veranda.

....

I saw two flies playing football in a saucer

So I asked what they were doing

They replied were practicing as they were playing in the cup tomorrow

....

When one door closes another one opens.

Apart from that it's a great car.

....

I was just watching Peppa Pig when my wife came in and turned the TV off.

How childish is that?

....

Scientists have discovered that this first two people on Earth were Cockneys. Would you Adam and Eve it.

....

My dryer door keeps popping open during use. If it does it one more time, that's it,

I'm throwing in the towel

....

I joined a club.

We criticize merlot, moan about sauvignon blanc, groan about Riesling and wail about chardonnay.

It a local Whine group.

I saw this bloke with a wheelbarrow full of rabbit's feet and four leaf clovers.

I thought...he's pushing his luck.

....
.

I got told off for Jumping up and down at a party.

I asked what the problem was, I'm trying to enjoy myself and I've taken my shoes off but apparently the bouncy castle was for under 5's

....

I've just had my Christmas dinner.

Those slow cookers are useless

....

There's a field on the north side of our valley that never gets any sun. I like to sit there and listen to 'Tubular Bells'.

It's my cold field.

....

I went to the local cinema last night. The man sat in front of me had his dog with him. The dog seemed really engrossed in the film. When the movie had ended, I said to the owner "This might seem weird, but you dog seemed to really like that film."

"Yes I thought that to" said the man "He hated the book!"

....

The Hunchback of Notre Dame retired today.

He received two years back pay, a lump sum, and a case of Bells.

....

For the first time since 1945 the National Spelling Bee has been cansul...cansil...cansell..

It's been called off.

118   I'll get my Jacket

....

So I went to the prehistoric museum in London today and asked the curator how old the Tyrannosaurus Rex skeleton was?

He said: "68 million and seven years old."

I said: "How can you be so accurate?"

He said: "When I started working here, they told me it was 68 million years old and I've been here 7 years."

I surprised a burglar once...

I broke into his house!!

....

My brother took me on holiday to see the Norwegian Fjords.

I was there for a week and didn't see a single Fiesta, Focus ,Escort or Cortina.

....

There have been reports of a robbery at the Agoraphobia Clinic.

The Police suspect it's an inside job.

....

In the old West they used to mount a lantern on their horses to help find their way at night.

It was the first known means of saddle light navigation.....

....

I hear they're building furniture stores on top of Kings Cross and St. Pancreas.

I think they're getting IKEA's above their station.

....

The Self Depreciation Society is inviting applications.

I've already put myself down!

....

Went to the DIY shop and had to go to the hospital after I fainted in the adhesive isle.

The Doctor said I'm glue tin intolerant

....

Elton John has got so fat, he's having to have his trousers specially made.

Goodbye normal jeans.

I recently entered a competition in an astronomy magazine.

I didn't win, but I got a constellation prize.

....

Cheryl Crow has a sister called Val.

She's constantly getting ripped off.

....

I've just lost my job at the bank.

It's a real shame, I was taking home £250,000 a week

....

In these hard times my friend has taken up cleaning roads after dark.

I don't know how he sweeps at night.

....

My wife is in A&E after being stung on the forehead by a Hornet. Her face is terribly bruised and she has a huge lump on her head.

Thankfully when the Hornet struck, I was close enough to hit it with a shovel.

I have a new girlfriend.

She works at a factory making wheelie bins.

Not sure what day to take her out.

...

A man walks into a bar. He reaches into his pocket and pulls out a little man, maybe a foot tall and a little piano. He puts them both on the bar, and the little guy starts playing Mozart as the man orders his drink.

The bartender says "I'm sure it's none of my business, but where did you find a little man who plays piano like that?"

The guy says "There's a genie outside granting wishes, I bet he's still there if you hurry."

The bartender runs outside, and moments later a bunch of ducks come in through the front door and start causing a big ruckus. The bartender says "You didn't tell me the genie was deaf, I asked for a million bucks, not a million ducks."

The guy says..

Do you really think I asked for an eleven inch pianist?"

I'll get my Jacket

So I went to a really trendy nightclub last night.

The doorman said to me "Sorry mate, I can't let you in, you've had too many!"

I said "What, drinks?"

He said "No, birthdays".

....

Facemasks can save lives. Yesterday a friend of

mine went out with his girlfriend and on the way to the mall he passed by his wife and she did not recognize him.

....

We were on Holiday in Dubai, where I was offered 40 camels for my wife. I normally smoke Marlboro, but hey, a deals a deal.

....

Bob had ran out of petrol, suddenly a Bee flew into his car

"Are you out of gas?" asked the bee.

"Yes" replied Bob.

"Gimme a minute" said the bee, and flew to the hive and returned with the hive of bees. They flew inside Bob's petrol tank. Moments later they flew out, when the bee said to Bob

"Try it now"

The car started first time, Bob said

"Wow, what did you put in the tank?"

The bee replied…wait for it!

BP

My mate told me that he failed his history of Aboriginal music exam.

I asked him, "Didya redo it?"

....

I just realized that I haven't done the "Hokey Cokey"" in over 10 years.

I guess when you get older, you just forget what it's all about.

....

The surface of the earth is approx 70% water. None of it is carbonated, thus proving the earth is flat.

....

Due to a typo, I was the only one to turn up to the inaugural meeting of the new pilates group without a wooden leg

I've just discovered that the fella who lives about halfway down our street is called Richard Rowse.

Does that make him....

R. Rowse, in the middle of our street?

....

This weekend I start on my 50th and final Marathon

Next week

MARS BARS

....

I Hate Russia doll's, there so full of themselves.

....

Looks like the idiots aren't confining themselves to petrol. The bloke who filled up before me then went into the shop and emptied the shelves of all the San Miguel and Sol Lager, the frozen paella ready meals and the Old El Paso fajita kits.

I thought to myself......Hispanic buying

....

I've just finished my first nude painting.

My neighbours weren't too happy about it, but the fence looks great

....

There are 4 questions. Do in order and don't miss one.

1. How do you put a giraffe into a refrigerator?

Stop and think about it and decide on your answer before you scroll down

Correct Answer: Open the refrigerator, put in the giraffe, and close the door.

This question tests whether you tend to do simple things in an overly complicated way.

2. How do you put an elephant into a refrigerator?

Did you say, open the refrigerator, put in the elephant, and close the refrigerator?

Wrong...

Correct Answer: Open the refrigerator, take out the giraffe, put in the elephant and close the door.

This tests your ability to think through the repercussions of your previous actions.

3. The Lion King is hosting an animal conference. All the animals attend... Except one.

Which animal does not attend?

Correct Answer : The elephant. The elephant is in the refrigerator. You just put him in there.

This tests your memory...

Okay, even if you did not answer the first three questions correctly, you still have one more chance to show your true abilities.

4. There is a river you must cross but it is used by crocodiles, and

you do not have a boat.

How do you manage it?

Correct Answer: You jump into the river and swim across. Have you not been listening? All the crocodiles are attending the Animal Meeting.

This tests whether you learn quickly from your mistake.

....

The Bible and the Quran both tells us to love one another.

The Kama Sutra however is a bit more specific.

....

Difficult things to say when Drunk:

1. Innovative.
2. Preliminary.
3. Cinnamon.

Very difficult things to say when drunk"

1. Specificity.
2. Passive-Disorder.
3. Transubstantiate.

Things that are downright impossible to say when drunk.

1. No thanks, I'm married.
2. No more for me thank you.
3. No, I don't want to see your tits.

....

A woman awakes during the night to find that her husband is not in bed. She puts on her robe and goes downstairs to look for him. She finds him sitting at the kitchen table with a hot cup of coffee in front of him. He appears to be in deep thought, just staring at the wall. She watches as he wipes a tear from his eye and takes a sip of his coffee.

'What's the matter, dear' she whispers as she steps into the room, 'Why are you down here at this time of night

The husband looks up from his coffee, 'It's the 20th Anniversary of the day we met'.

She can't believe he has remembered and starts to tear up.

The husband continues, 'Do you remember 20 years ago when we started dating, I was 18 and you were only 16,' he says solemnly.

Once again, the wife is touched to tears. 'Yes, I do' she replies.

The husband pauses The words were not coming easily. 'Do you remember when your father caught us in the back seat of my car'

'Yes, I remember' said the wife, lowering herself into the chair beside him.

The husband continued. 'Do you remember when he shoved the shotgun in my face and said, "Either you marry my daughter or I will send you to prison for 20 years'

'I remember that, too' she replied softly.

He wiped another tear from his cheek and said "I would have gotten out today."

....

My Wife said I never buy her flowers.

I didn't even know she sold flowers.

....

I decided to cover myself in bubble wrap this morning for a laugh.

The wife had a right go at me. And now the rest of my family are having a pop.

....

Me: "Alexa remind me to go to the Gym."

Alexa: "I have added Gin to your shopping list."

Me: "Close enough!"

....

Things Confucius DID NOT say:

Man who wants pretty Nurse must be patient.

Passionate kiss, like spider web, leads to undoing of fly.

Squirrel who runs up lady leg will not find nuts.

A lion will not cheat on his wife, but a Tiger wood.

Man who fish in another man's well, often catch crabs.

Man who live in glasshouse, must change his clothes in Basement.

It takes many nails to make a crib. But one screw to fill it.

Man who fight with wife all day, get no piece at night.

War does not determine who is right, only who is left.

....

Four CEOs of beer companies are having a meeting and decide to get a drink.

The CEO of Budweiser orders a Bud Light.

The CEO of Miller orders a Miller Light.

The CEO of Coors orders a Coors Light.

The CEO of Guinness orders a Coke.

The other three CEOS ask him "Why aren't you ordering Guinness""

He replies "If you guys are not drinking beer, then neither will I."

....

A recent study showed that Men around the World aged between 40 to 60 will have sex around 2 to 3 times a week (Some a little bit more). Whereas Japanese men in the same age group will have sex 2 to 3 times a year, if they are lucky.

This study has shocked many of my friends as they had no idea they were Japanese.

....

My Doctor has told me I need to stop drinking. This will be a big change for me.

I've been with that Doctor for 25 years.

....

I saw an old man with a fishing pole trying to catch fish in a puddle, outside my local bar. He looked so cold. I took pity on him and took him into the bar.

We were enjoying our double whiskies, I opened up the chat with "How many have you caught today?"

He replied "You are the 8th."

Woke up this morning and there was a big piece of plasticine on my pillow.

I didn't know what to make of it.

A man dressed in a white rodent costume has been seen mugging women at knife point.

Police have warned people not to approach the suspect as he's armed and Dangermouse.

I've just bought a second hand watch!

Now I can see the minutes as well as the hours.

I've just started the Adam Ant diet

Don't chew ever, don't chew ever....

I joined Weight Watchers and rang them and said it was an emergency and could they send someone round.

They said, "No problem, we've got loads of those".

....

When in service Gran's job was to wake the Master's children up in the morning by making fun of them.

She was a Tease maid.

....

I saw a girl last night with twelve breasts, sounds unbelievable dozen tit.

....

Scientists have discovered that trees have a way of communicating with each other.

It's called What Sap

....

If I'm reading their lips correctly...

My neighbors are arguing about some creepy guy next door.

....

Did you know that soul singer Bill Withers had a brother called 'Bear' who wrote telephone hold music?

....

My wife left me because I am obsessed with becoming a supermarket cashier.

I asked her if she wanted any help with her packing…

....
.

I was once in a band called "The Heaters" we were a warm-up act.

Then I joined "The Blankets" we were a cover act.

After that, I started "Cats Eyes" we played middle of the road stuff.

Now I'm in a group called "Missing Cat" you may have seen our posters!

....

News just in.

There have been reports of cannibalism at a convent near Coventry.

Nuneaton

I went on Dragons Den the other night and showed them my Dads old shotgun.

Peter Jones said "And what's your idea?"

I replied "It's a simple concept Peter, just put the money in the bag

A coach load of jazz musicians has just overturned on the M1.

Expect lengthy jams.

I dated an anesthetist once.

It didn't last long, I just didn't feel anything.

- I went to Europe to watch Teletubbies fly airplanes.

- "Poland?"

- "Yes, they all did."

I'll get my Jacket

My cat just swallowed a £2 coin, I was going take it to the vets but my wife said, "Don't bother, there's not enough money in the kitty."

....

Bill Smith the well-known receiver of stolen goods tragically died today.

He fell off the back of a lorry.

....

just to let you all know, I've been admitted to Hospital. I've just gone and poisoned myself. I ate what I thought was an onion but it was a Daffodil Bulb. They said I'll be out sometime in the Spring.

....

What was the main difference between King Arthur and Cleopatra?

Arthur had Camelot and Cleopatra had lots of Camels.

....

Off for a lovely little break in Cornwall.

Not sure why my boss stipulated I should take my time off in Looe, but I'm sure he knows best.

....

My wife is threatening to leave me because she thinks I'm too old fashioned!

I'll wager a groat she's courting another gentleman.

....

So since my neighbour got out of prison he got a job repairing bent archery equipment.

He's on the straighten arrow now!

....

I changed my bed from a King size to a Queen size but now I've got shivers down my spine, body's aching all the time! ...

....

Julie Andrews has stopped endorsing her lipstick brand as it crumbles easily and makes her breath smell.

In a statement issued today she said,

"The super colour fragile lipstick gives me Halitosis "

....
...

I've heard that the local prosthetics shop is changing hands.

....

A lion wearing sunglasses is at a bar. Absolutely nobody notices the lion!

The Eagles band spot it within seconds.

Why?

Because according to them, "You can't hide your Lion eyes"

....

Police say a man who held people hostage in a bowling alley, is likely to strike again

....

Women do better Black Country accents than men, because the female of the species is more Dudley than the male.

....

I see Cheryl Baker from Bucks Fizz got her car stuck for hours in the snow last night.

In case you don't know, to move a car stuck in the snow, first you gotta speed it up, then you gotta slow it down.

I'm surprised she didn't know that.

....

Had a guy working in our warehouse called Vincent.

He painted the pallets blue and grey.

....

I'm so upset. Deliveroo dropped my curry and ruined the side dish. It's my chapati and I'll cry if I want to.

....

To watch the latest Nuclear weapons tests on the BBC, press the red button now.

....
.

Many years ago I rented a flat, the landlady said "I hope you've got a good memory for faces" When I asked why, she said "There's no mirror in the bathroom"

....

I'm so lazy I've got a smoke alarm with a snooze button

Looking for an expert to lecture on pachyderm pregnancy but no one wants to talk about the elephant in the womb.

....

I asked the waiter if anyone ever sent a steak back for being undercooked.

He said 'It's very rare'.

....

Some scumbag has just pinched a tree from out of our garden. Bring back the Birch l say

....

Just found out my dad used to be a mime artist .... He kept that quiet.

....

Elton John just saw his flip flop get blown away

He said it was like a sandal in the wind

....

My secret plans for the Best Kept Garden in the Village are ruined.

I think we have a mole.

....

If fireworks pass their sell-by date do they go off?

....

I want to sell all my John Lennon stuff on eBay.

Imagine all the PayPal

....

My wife is always stealing my t-shirts and sweaters.

But if I take one of her dresses, suddenly "we need to talk"

....

Audi are about to release their friendliest model yet.

It's going to be called the Audi do.

....

I found a bottle washed up on the seashore

There was a message from Sting

....

I bought a Memory foam mattress and now it's trying to blackmail me

....

I'm constantly being followed by a woman dressed as a tub of margarine,

I think I'm being storked.

....

Rod Stewart has been filling in potholes near his house. He told reporters that....

'The first rut was the deepest'.

....

Thanks for all the good wishes but I'm ok.

We just got back from the hospital after a long night.

They reckon I might have pneumonoultramicroscopicsilicovolcanoconiosis but at the moment it's hard to say.

A little boy kills a butterfly; his Father tells him 'No butter for two weeks.'

The little boy later kills a Honeybee: His Father tells him 'No honey for two weeks.'

The little boy's Mother kills a cockroach, the little boy turns to his Father and says

'Are you gonna tell her or shall I?'

....

While visiting a cathedral in Paris, I bought 7 bananas from a street vendor outside....when I dropped a few he offered me a large elastic band to keep them all together.....

I thought. "This must be the famous 'Bunch Hack of Notre Dame'

....

Fred Flintstone: I've got a problem with my car.

Chiropodist: Let's take a look.

....

First, ancient man started using bronze; that was the Bronze Age. Then they started using Iron; that was the Iron Age.

Then man discovered the benefits of a fibre diet.

that was the Rough age.

....
.

With the weather getting warmer I've started a magazine about ice cream.

I've just had my first scoop.

....

I'm really disgusted with myself...I was on the verge of winning the "World's Most Congested Nose" competition ...and I blew it!

....

Had to go into the hospital for a cardiac x-ray.

The doc said, "We can see a shell, a head and four flippers. As we thought, you have a turtle eclipse of the heart."

....

So I'm not happy because I have to work at the museum tonight moving suits of armour.

I hate knight shifts.

....

"Dad, can you tell me what happens during an eclipse?"

"No son"

....

I went to an interesting 'Evening with Anthony Hopkins the world famous actor the other day.

It was a Hannibal Lecture.

....

My girlfriend had been under the doctor for the last few months.

That's one of the reasons he was struck off.

....

I was shown around an empty perfume factory today.

It made no scents whatsoever.

....
.

I tried to get John Milton's most famous poem from the library but they couldn't find it.

....

When I die I want to be buried with all my LP records…. It will be my vinyl resting place

....

Did you know that Napoleons remains are buried in St Helena but his skull is on display in a Parisian museum.

I think it's a shame to keep Napoleon's Bones apart.

....

My wife will be on the plane now.

Holiday?

No, she's taking half an inch off the bottom of the kitchen door.

....

When I worked as a doctor, my colleague really annoyed me by sending messages to the people that I was diagnosing.

He was really texting my patients.

....

If I had a hammer, I'd hammer in the morning, I'd hammer in the evening, all over this land.

I'm not allowed a hammer.

....

I'm making a documentary series on aviation.

We're currently filming the pilot.

....

My friend recently creosoted my front porch without permission. I told him never to darken my door again.

....

When teaching history about the conquests I rely on Norman Wisdom

....

Has the Imperial War Museum gone metric yet?

....

A man has died from 3rd degree burns over most of his body.

Apparently he called 999 to report his pants were on fire, but they thought he was lying.

....
.

It turns out when asked who your favourite child is, you're supposed to pick one of your own!

I know that now!

....

Tried to warn my mate about the dangers of Russian Roulette,

but it went straight in one ear and out the other!

....

The worst pub I ever went to was called "The Fiddle".

It was a vile inn

....

I'm looking for a one-night stand ladies.

I have nothing to put my other bedside lamp on

....

Ever got out of the shower and your bathroom mirror has not been steamed up?

You could be entitled to condensation.

....

I've been trying to grow plants in my plastic alligator, but it didn't work- I'm now using a propergator.

....

Just going out to take my Dogfish for a walk.I've been doing that since he was a guppy

....

I was out last night when I saw a bird of prey, singing Enola Gay and darting back and forth in search of a meal.

I assumed it was either an hallucination or Kestral Manoeuvres in the Dark.

....

I shortened the rope on the bucket they use to collect water in the village.

Didn't go down well.

....

Anyone know where I can get fresh ice cubes?

I don't want any of those frozen ones!

....
.

When my Wife said she'd tampered with my parachute I hit the roof.

....

John Denver is coming over to my house on Sunday April 3rd. He's going to fill up my census.

I find that giving someone you care about either a watch or clock as a gift, is the ultimate in thoughtfulness.

As the saying goes: there's no present like the time.

....

Every time I pick my letters for Scrabble, I get a rumbly tummy....and I always pick only A's - E's - I's - O's and U's

The doctor thinks I've got irritable vowel syndrome

....

I'm going to a fancy dress party dressed as Anne Boleyn.

I'll beheading off soon.

....

Fell asleep last night reading old magazines.

Woke up this morning with back issues.

....

Quite emotional retiring from my job at the auctioneers and bidding farewell to my colleagues.

Scientists say it's now possible to live on Mars.

I tried it for 3 months and put on 2 stone!

....

I had a date last night. I Really enjoyed it.

Tonight, I'm going to try a fig.

....

The local tax office is on fire.

Don't panic, I've written to the fire brigade

....

I took my new girlfriend home to meet my dad, after saying hello my dad pulled me to one side and said bloody hell son you could have done a lot better than that. She's cross eyed fat she's got a beard and she stinks. I said there's no need to whisper dad she's deaf.

....

Orthodontists are going on strike.

Brace yourselves.

For health reasons I do prefer milk in cartons that have previously been bounced across a body of water….

I threw a ball for my dog. I know it was a bit extravagant, but it was his birthday and he looked great in a tuxedo.

A Scottish friend of mine sings in a Swedish tribute band called ABBA Dean.

My doctor rang me the other day and told me my DNA was backwards,

I replied, "AND?'

My aunt has been in hospital recently. She's doing okay and has been passing the time by playing board games such as backgammon, draughts and mah-jongg.

"Any chess?"

"No, she went private".

I went back to the doctor and told him the pile cream he gave me caused a very nasty

reaction.

He said where did you apply it .

I said on the bus.

....

I lost my balance on an escalator and fell down the stairs for 2 hours

....

Deaf sheepdogs...they're hard to come by

....

My wife has left me as she says I'm obsessed with compasses.

She was last seen heading North North West.

....

I can type a short message on my phone - using either hand.

I'm ambitexterous!

Priscilla saw Elvis getting back out of the swimming pool for the 10th time.

She asked what he was doing.

He said, "I can't help falling in, love."

....

A fight between staff at the local Royal Mail depot nearly broke out but the managers told the staff to sort it.

....

I first met my girlfriend on a village green! There were marquees, food stalls, tug of war and a tombola..

Fete brought us together

....

I was going to cook alligator stew but then realized I only had a croc pot

....

I worked in an optician's but I fell into the lens grinder and made a spectacle of myself.

I worked at the zoo making a sort of soup for the hyenas. It was mixed in a big caldron. When I was stirring it I leaned over a little bit too far, fell in and became a laughing stock.

....

I worked in a suppository factory. Couldn't get on with any of my co-workers.

I made a lot of enemas there.

....

Stealing clothes from washing lines... been there, done that, got the T-shirt....

....

I'd put £5 each way on the Dalali Lama if I was a Tibetan man.

....

The gorillas in the zoo live in abject poverty.

They don't have two ape knees to rub together

....

I just found my mate slumped over Hadrian's Wall with an empty vodka bottle in his hand.

I think he might be a borderline alcoholic.

....

I have to give a speech on the link between anxiety and insomnia next week…

I've been up all night worrying about it

....

I'll never forget what my late uncle said to me.

He said, "I'm sorry I'm late."

....

My Girlfriend bought lots of Impressionist paintings, but very little Chanel Number 5.

Seems to me like she's got more Monet than scents.

....

I've just started a new diet. I look at people serving food instead of eating it.

It's called Watch Waiters.

....

Did you know that the blue whale is so huge that if you put it end to end on a football pitch, the match would have to be cancelled.

....

As I walked into my local shop the other day, some bloke attacked me with some milk, cheese, yogurt and cream..

I thought 'How Dairy?'

....

The Dutch inventor of the inflatable shoe has sadly popped his clogs.

....

Rumours of a food shortage at the annual spoonerism awards turned out to be a lack of pies.

....

My book, 'How To Say No Emphatically In German', now available - only £9.99!

....

I bought the most modern type of garden shears today.

Apparently they are the latest cutting hedge technology

My wife said, "I'm of your obsession with wanting to be a detective. I think we should split up.

split up."

I said, "Good idea. We can cover more ground that way."

....

A clown held the door open for me, when he saw me carrying heavy shopping in town today.

My immediate thought was "What a nice jester".

....

I was doing fine getting home from the pub then somebody trod on my fingers

....

Wife; "Did you know that Butterflies only live for 24 hours?"

Me; "Surely that's a myth!"

Wife; "Nope. it's definitely a Butterfly!"

....

Biting insects have been driving my pig mad.

Midge over troubled snorter.

....

Before the iron age, did people just walk around wearing creased clothes?

....

just heard that in the English Channel, a ship carrying red paint has collided with a ship carrying purple paint. It is believed that both crews have been marooned.

....

I popped into the library and asked if they had any books on coincidences.

The librarian said, "As a matter of fact, this one's just arrived"

....

Friend of mine sprinted down to the chemist and bought the first skin cream he could see - didn't even ask the price.

Rash.

....

As a painter I'm proud to say that some of my work is on show at the National Gallery.

I did the skirting boards.

....

Can't believe it took me 15 years of using anti dandruff shampoo before I realized doing the shoulders was optional.

....

A soldier who was renting my house has done a runner owing me 6 months rent!!

He told me he was a General but I've since discovered he's a Left Tenant

....

I'm not saying lady in front of me at the checkout in Tescos had bad teeth but when she smiled, the barcode scanner picked it up as a set of saucepans.

....

There was a tragic accident at the cake factory; a worker fell in to a huge vat of fruit cake mix; he almost avoided drowning, but sadly, he was pulled under by a strong currant.

....

I wish I'd bought my baked beans online.

Heinz site's a wonderful thing.

....

I was watching the television, when the wife walked past and turned it off. After sitting there for an hour staring at a blank screen, I thought to myself...

That's not on.

....

I can't help being lazy.

It walks in the family.

....

Congratulations to Hugh Zappriti Boyden who has been elected president of the British Budgerigar Society.

....

I really thought my wife was joking when she said she wanted to see a Monkees tribute band in Switzerland.

Then I saw her face, now I'm in Geneva.

....

In Germany does a cat have no lives?

....

After years of research, I am about to launch my 100 calorie pizza.

Guaranteed to not make you fat!

This has earned me a nomination for a no belly pizza prize

....

I had to give up the job of tree surgeon.

I couldn't stand the sight of sap.

....

I went to the doctors today and I said: "I feel like I've got some cutlery stuck in my throat." The doc had a look and said: "It's not serious, you just need to have utensils taken out."

....

My local dentist is an opera singer.

He has a falsetto teeth.

Apparently the billionaire boss of Amazon has left his wife.

Presumably with a neighbour.

....

Engineers have made a car that can run on Parsley.

Now they are hoping that they can make buses and trains run on thyme.

....

A friend of mine wears a very minimal swimsuit to go swimming every evening.

Just a thong at twilight.

....

My dog's getting slow in his old age.

I sent him down to the news agents.

He's just brought me yesterday's newspaper.

....

I replied "No comment" to every question in a police interview.

I didn't get the job

....

I have a friend who used to row for Oxford, he was in the debating society.

....

When I was growing up, plastic surgery was a bit of a taboo subject.

These days if you mention Botox no one raises an eyebrow.

....

My wife said she didn't believe I was a proper cockney so I stormed up the apples and oranges!!!

....

My mate who is into fishing, uses liquorice as bait. He says he catches all sorts.

....

My brother and I inherited some furniture from the local zoo.

I'm glad to say I got the lion's chair.

Did you hear about the policeman who was only 4 foot five tall?

His Sargent said he wasn't much cop

....

Lost my mother in law last night.... what a game of cards that was!

....

Ever since I drew a watch on my wrist with a ballpoint pen, I've been living on biroed time.

....

In the 2nd World War, my Grand dad got his back bone shot up. As a repair the Medics put Mercury in it. That was ok, in the Summer he was six-foot three, but in the winter he was five-foot six .

Now That is all to deliver, I am guessing my Jacket is over there then

****

About the Author

Steven William Park

Steven William Park, 65, served 25 years in Her Britannic Majesty's Royal Navy, serving on both ships and Diesel Submarines. He also spent 20 years working on Cruise ships. A total of 45 years as a Mariner and is now retired.

Other works by Steve Park:

A Magical Balloon ride
The Intrepid Six
The Adult Joke book

www.ingramcontent.com/pod-product-compliance
Lightning Source LLC
LaVergne TN
LVHW041840070526
838199LV00045BA/1360